GilChrist

GilChrist

A Place to Remember

Molly Vass-Lehman

BROWN BOOKS
PUBLISHING GROUP

GilChrist
A Place to Remember

Brown Books Publishing Group
Dallas, TX / New York, NY
www.BrownBooks.com
(972) 381-0009

A New Era in Publishing®

Publisher's Cataloging-In-Publication Data

Names: Vass-Lehman, Molly, author.
Title: GilChrist : a place to remember / Molly Vass-Lehman.
Description: Dallas, TX ; New York, NY : Brown Books Publishing Group, [2023]
Identifiers: ISBN: 978-1-61254-657-5 (hardcover)
Subjects: LCSH: GilChrist (Organization) | Spiritual retreat centers--Michigan. | Spiritual healing.
Classification: LCC: BL2527.M5 V37 2023 | DDC: 206.509774--dc23

ISBN 978-1-61254-657-5
LCCN 2023944567

Printed in China
10 9 8 7 6 5 4 3 2 1

For more information or to contact the author, please go to
www.GilChristRetreatCenter.org.

To the courageous individuals who seek to live in greater harmony with all of creation, may you find ways and places like GilChrist to help you on your journey.

Contents

Going home

Preface

*"There's a thread you follow. It goes among
things that change. But it doesn't change.
People wonder about what you are pursuing.
You have to explain about the thread.
But it is hard for others to see.
While you hold it you can't get lost.
Tragedies happen; people get hurt
or die: and you suffer and get old.
Nothing you can do can stop time's unfolding.
You don't ever let go of the thread."*

—**WILLIAM STAFFORD**
The Way It Is: New & Selected Poems[1]

Life is often not what we expect. How we end up where we do is beyond reason and imagination. This is a story about following a call too mysterious to understand, but when propelled by love, you must follow and hopefully can hang on to the thread. This journey not only led to an unimagined place but also allowed us to travel back home to our hearts.

Humans are seekers by nature. Travelling inwardly and outwardly, we are changed by experiences. Whether one finds a sacred place such as a retreat center, monastery, or special place in nature, it is important to learn to listen to one's inner voice and remember what is essential. Taking time out of our busy and sometimes overwhelming lives can help us bring a better balance and perspective, one of compassion and love, to those around us. The longing for a deeper connection to ourselves, the earth, and others lies in our own human heart. The world we live in now is calling desperately for healing, for us to bring our light to create greater peace and love. It is important to be able to listen to ourselves carefully so we may respond thoughtfully to the issues in our own lives and the world around us. Whether we are struggling with relationships or a decision about our work lives or health issues, times of retreat and reflection allow the noise and busyness of the world to fall away so we can hear our innermost thoughts and desires.

My husband Rob and I could never have imagined that our journey would lead us to create a retreat center and build a small stone chapel that others, like ourselves, would come to seek peace and beauty from for so many years.

We named the retreat center after Sister GilChrist, a Trappist nun who inspired us to build an interfaith retreat center. She took this name when she joined a monastery because of the richness of its meaning in different languages. In Persian, GilChrist means "flower;" in Hebrew, "joy;" in old English, "rivulet" or "stream;" and in Irish, "servant of Christ." In his book *Lord of the Rings: The Return of the King*, Tolkien referred to the name as the "star" or "epiphany."[2] We felt the name was appropriate, as it has as many diverse meanings as the diversity of people who find their way here. GilChrist is an interfaith retreat center and also a place for people of no particular faith or a faith in nature. It is for all those seeking a sense of the sacred in their lives.

We could not have foreseen that, in 2023, we would have lived through the COVID-19 pandemic, witnessed a climate crisis, and be living in a divided country. For so many during this time, there is a feeling of isolation, uncertainty, loneliness, and despair. These emotions are bringing an urgency for individuals to seek ways and places to restore a sense of peace and beauty in their lives. Trying not to fall into fear, anger, and hopelessness, people are going out into nature and finding outlets such as mindfulness, meditation, and prayer. They are going to retreat centers, monasteries, and sacred sites. Now more than ever, places like GilChrist are essential to helping individuals recover a sense of the sacred in their everyday lives. When the problems seem overwhelming and decisions in our life feel monumental, it is hard to calm down, gain perspective, and know how to handle what is in front of us. The need to step away from our everyday lives demands slowing down and reflecting before moving forward, and places like GilChrist provide the silence, solitude, and support for these times in our lives.

Whether it is a health crisis, loss of a loved one, or a major decision about our life or work, it is crucial to come into relationship with these decisions in the most thoughtful way possible: a walk in the woods, the sound of the wind, prairie grasses swaying—these can bring us back to the natural world around us. Witnessing the sunrise and sunset, seeing a doe and its fawn, or watching a butterfly lightly land on a milkweed plant can bring us into the moment to witness the beauty around us and the larger universe that enfolds us. In living simply, we begin to place our awareness on ordinary things around us and see them in a new light. The beauty of a flame in the fire or a flower in the field outside our window can transport us to a larger experience of life that we are so intimately interconnected with.

Before his death, John O'Donohue spoke of times like this in his book *Beauty*.

> *"In a sense, all the contemporary crisis can*
> *be reduced to a crisis of beauty. The Greek word*
> *for 'the beautiful' is 'to kalon,' related to the word*
> *kalein, which includes the notion of 'call.' When*
> *we experience beauty, we feel called. Even amidst*
> *chaos and disorder, something in the human*
> *mind continues still to seek beauty."*[3]

When we lose a sense of beauty, we do not care for others, ourselves, or the earth. We forget what is true and cannot see or listen for what is most important. Some people find that through art, music, or literature, they are transported into a new way of seeing or hearing that elevates them out of their ordinary experience. Others find these transformative and awe-inspiring experiences by being in nature. We come back from these

Prairie grasses, sunlight, and mist

moments with a greater ability to see the beauty in our own lives and the world around us and a greater commitment to caring for these things. We can see the beauty in the faces of those we love and the things in our life that are vital and nourishing.

Anne Frank wrote in her diary about being able to see the branches of a tree and how that helped to keep her hope alive. In her diary, she wrote:

> *"The best remedy for those who are frightened, lonely, or unhappy is to go outside:*
> *somewhere they can be alone, alone with the sky, nature, and God. For then and*
> *only then can you feel that everything is as it should be."* [4]

Individuals experiencing even the most horrendous events and sudden tragedies can still have the freedom to find meaning and beauty in the moments of their days. Some lives are short and others long, some with an unexpected injury causing a disability or great health challenges like cancer, multiple sclerosis, a stroke, addictions, or dementia. There are courageous individuals who have found ways to breathe peace and joy into the moments of their days, even amidst the realities of their situation. I have seen this with friends and family and also with many people that have come to GilChrist out of a need to rest from the exhausting task of caring for others and keeping up with the pace of life. They desire to clear their minds and to feel cared for amidst the beauty of nature. This experience can bring a sense of a connection to something larger, more eternal, in their life and help them connect to a deeper meaning and purpose. They also find others with similar challenges and share in a newfound community, supporting each other through difficult times. Stepping away from our lives for time in contemplation allows us to understand that we do not have control over the events or individuals in our lives, but we do have the choice and responsibility to live the best we can with compassion and love for ourselves and others.

Tree of Hope

Resting in nature

The Laura

Chapter 1

The Call

"Today I find that I am the person who has left home and who has lost the key to get myself back there. Benedict, your message is an invitation to interiority. Your experience is that of a person who regains their sense of themselves. Benedict, teach us to return to the heart."

—Esther de Waal
A Life-Giving Way: A Commentary on the Rule of St. Benedict[1]

There are times in our life when we can hear a whisper to the heart, a siren call to the soul. Although imperceptible to the mind, somehow, the heart follows. Why we are called out of our ordinary lives to somewhere beyond our imagination is a mystery. What grace allows us to listen to something we know, but cannot remember, calling us back home?

This is a story about a place that feels out of ordinary time, surrounded by nature, in silence and solitude. A place to remember who we are and what we want in our lives. People are drawn to discover a simpler, more meaningful way to live. It is about the seasons of our lives and how we find hope to meet the challenges that come in our life cycle. It is also about the love we find along the way.

Like most love stories, it began with two people. One Sunday afternoon, they went for a jog on a country road in Three Rivers, Michigan, and ended up building a

Sacred land

contemplative retreat center. The unlikely story began thirty-three years ago, or more likely, long before they arrived.

The Potawatomi, Peoria, and other indigenous people inhabited the rural area of southwestern Michigan—filled with prairie grasses, an abundance of wildlife, and natural springs flowing from three rivers. They believed there were great spirits all around them in the earth and sky. People from other parts of the country migrated to this area seeking a new life in the beauty and fertility of this place.

It is easy to see why, over the last eighty years, religious and spiritual communities gravitated here. It was a place set apart from the busyness of life where one could experience silence and solitude and feel the presence of nature and spirit all around.

The first to come was a community of Benedictine monks, followed by a Jungian community and a Mennonite retreat center. These places provided a space for others to make pilgrimages out of their ordinary lives for times of contemplation and prayer. These communities shared the values of simplicity, silence, and helping each other care for the land, along with offering the space for people seeking out places for prayer, contemplation, and the experience of nature.

Rob and I found our way there, and it changed the course of our lives. Like many others, our lives were overwhelmingly busy with work, travel, and relationships. Rob was President of the Fetzer Institute, a nonprofit foundation with a mission at the time of bringing credibility to the emerging field of mind/body health through education and science. My work was as a consultant, a private-practice therapist, professor and director of a university holistic health care program, and founding fellow of the Fetzer Institute. All of these roles required enormous time and energy as we helped to find the best experts in the field and to create programs all over the country in educational and healthcare settings. It was important work, and we were working diligently and tirelessly to keep up with all the great possibilities and potential. We were also learning about how important this new information and practice could be to people's health and well-being. Meeting the experts and practitioners in the fields was inspiring, but we needed to find a way to navigate a life so full of responsibilities, knowing that the more we did, the more opportunities were possible.

The mission of the Institute was important, and we felt compelled to bring the ideas out into the mainstream culture. Our lives, like others, could easily spin out of control. Finding a balance would be essential. As a person teaching and counseling others about the importance of these approaches, I knew that I was having less time and attention to these daily practices in my own life. If we did not take time out to pause and reflect, we could lose track of listening to our true selves and the greater wisdom around us. Fortunately, through our work, we were introduced to men and women who

Calming reflection

lived contemplative lives and introduced us to monastic contemplative practices. Their sense of peace, joy, and love was inspiring; we knew we needed to find a place to go, to take some time out periodically and bring greater balance to our lives.

We did not know that our need for a place to rest and renew was shared by so many others who needed a place as well. At the time, we could not have even imagined that part of our own journey moving to the country to live next to a Benedictine monastery would lead to us building a place for others. We also could have never foreseen the challenging times we would be living through, with the COVID-19 pandemic and overwhelming challenges in the world, and how much fear, anxiety, loss, and hopelessness this would bring to so many people. The necessity for places like GilChrist and other retreat centers would become more essential than ever.

As is often the case, there are many unseen events that weave the path of our lives to unexpected places. This is true of our journey to Three Rivers and the creation of GilChrist. It seemed unlikely that Rob (with Methodist roots) and I (of Scottish ancestry with Buddhist interests at the time) would end up interested in Christian monastic traditions and traveling to monasteries all over the United States and in Europe. We were astonished and amazed to find that our lives were changing in ways that seemed unlikely—a journey we could never have imagined.

One Sunday in July over thirty years ago, Rob and I decided to go to St. Gregory's Abbey in Three Rivers, Michigan, for one of the seven services the monks pray each day. We felt a great sense of comfort and peace hearing the ancient psalms chanted by the monks in a small, beautiful chapel—in the same way as monks have done since the fourteenth century. We knew this was something we wanted to experience more in our lives and made a commitment to come to the services as often as we could.

Afterwards, we went for a jog in the countryside surrounding the Abbey. A few miles out, it became apparent that we were lost and could not find our way back. We tried to reorient ourselves but to no avail. We ended up over two miles out and in front of a long dirt driveway that appeared to be a private residence, yet also might lead back towards the Abbey. Rob was sure it was a shortcut and ran uphill a quarter of a mile while I waited impatiently at the entrance of the driveway. When he returned, I learned that he had run around the house and surprised the residents, a couple sitting on their back deck. He ran around their back yard, waved, and headed back down the driveway. I was tired and not amused, so we headed back down the road to retrace our route and eventually found our way back to the Abbey.

Jogging after attending a service at the Abbey became a regular Sunday ritual. We became familiar with a route from the Abbey to Long Lake, which was a few miles away. A few Sundays after the first time we went for a run, we ran by the driveway with the dirt road again and there was a "For Sale" sign beside the mailbox. Rob was very excited and said that if the house property connected to the paths at the Abbey, we should buy it. He felt it would be wonderful to walk to the services as often as possible. Rob, being a man who loves ideas and had the romantic one of a house in nature next to the Abbey, thought this would be perfect.

As much as I loved going to the Abbey and knew we needed a greater commitment to our spiritual lives, the idea of buying a house with sixteen acres of land in the country forty-five minutes from work seemed unthinkable. With my practical nature, all that I could see was the complexity this would add to having jobs with great responsibility, traveling around the United States and Europe working for the Institute, along with time for relationships with family and friends . . .

Several weeks after we saw the "For Sale" sign, Rob suggested we try to walk from the back of the Abbey property to see where it would lead. The monastery logs parts of their forest to help support the monks' livelihood. Logging for the first time in forty years, the monastery had created a new path directly to the back of the house. Rob's arguments for all of the possibilities that a life in nature would bring—making paths, walking to services, and living in a place of great silence and beauty—were compelling. I knew the busyness and noise of our lives were not sustainable in the long run with our knowledge of how important deep spiritual connections and practices were for our health and well-being. Ultimately, the pull toward a life grounded in values of contemplation, prayer, and communion with nature helped me make the decision to take the leap of faith and hope this would be a good decision over time.

We were able to move out of our apartments and buy the house. By October, we were living in the woods in Three Rivers, beginning to reorient our life outside of work to a simpler one on the land with two newly adopted rescue cats, Martin Buber and Abbey.

Life has a way of surprising us. As we look back, we can see the pieces of the puzzle that came together over time. Sometimes we embrace the change that surprise brings, and sometimes we resist the dance. Part of our spiritual journey is coming to understand that surprise is not always part of our plan and is often part of a larger unseen order. We spent several years walking the land, creating paths, and walking to the Abbey to sit in the small chapel. This helped us to remember the things that were essential in our overly busy lives. As important as our work seemed, it could not be the center of our lives, and it needed to flow out of a place of greater balance and peace.

The journey home

> *"This is the space where the voice of God became audible, where that tranquility which the world cannot give waits to comfort the mind. People have come into this house with burdens of heart that could find healing nowhere else in the world. They have come for shelter when storms have unraveled every stitch of meaning from their lives. And they have come in too to give thanks for blessings and gifts they could never have earned."*
>
> —JOHN O'DONOHUE
> *To Bless the Space Between Us: A Book of Blessings*[2]

A place of prayer and healing

Our first winter in Three Rivers, we built a small hermitage (a place for solitary retreat and reflection) called Heathewood where I could do my psychotherapy and spiritual counseling, which was mostly with women going through major life transitions who had a deep desire to reconnect with their inner selves and something larger spiritually. They could stay for a time to reflect and rest in the hermitage and walk the land. I was not sure if my clients would make the effort to drive down to the woods in Three Rivers, but they did, one by one. As people sought a short time out of their overwhelming lives, over time more than we could accommodate came to us.

We had no intention of building a retreat center until a chance meeting with Sister GilChrist from Our Lady of Mississippi Abbey. Through our work with the Fetzer Institute, we were hosting a retreat on monastic values in everyday life at the Institute. The retreatants came for a weekend to live the

Our first hermitage

daily rhythm of a monk or nun and experience a life devoted to contemplation, prayer, and community. During a break, Sister GilChrist and I sat on the dock by the lake to process how we felt the experience was going for the retreatants. She spoke of the need for lay monastic retreat centers where others could come to have these experiences, a place that would provide support for individuals of any faith, or no faith, to try to bring sacred values into their ordinary lives and relationships. Out of the conversation, the idea for a place like GilChrist was born.

It took several years before all of the pieces fell into place to make this a reality. There were many twists and turns in the circuitous route to building GilChrist. At any turn, it looked as if it might not happen. Like the theme in the movie *Sliding Doors* in which the lead character played by Gwyneth Paltrow misses getting in the door of a subway and it alters the course of her life, each of us can look back and remember a moment where a decision we made changed the course of our life. The odds were against the building of a retreat center. We had to raise the money to set up a non-profit, find a builder we could afford, and secure land to ensure that the area would be free of noise and safe, as the land adjacent to us had been used by hunters for many years. Many times we felt the door was closed and the obstacles seemed insurmountable. And yet, one by one over several years, doors opened and each piece fell into place. Each time I was discouraged in the process, someone or something would come along to help make it possible.

Most of the time, I was kicking and screaming, saying, "I don't think we can do this." Yet, it kept moving along with Rob and I barely hanging on. Living on the land and going to the Abbey was the experience that anchored us to keep moving forward, along with the encouragement of those around us.

We had no idea what we were getting ourselves into. Like parents, if they knew up front all that would be asked of them, few would immediately volunteer for the job. It seems like all labors of love require challenges and sacrifices greater than we can imagine. The building of GilChrist—like the birth of a child or a creation of a piece of art or music—had all of the tribulations as well as joy and gratitude that is inherent in the process. Rob and I joked that we had to get married in 1994 because we were having a baby called GilChrist, and little did we know what a commitment this would require from us after we were married to care for the retreat center along with all of our other professional work. Giving my time to assist the retreatants, clean the cabins, and take care of Windhill (the meeting house), along with Rob making and clearing all the paths, was a labor of love. It was more than we could do alone for very long. Fortunately once again, people came and asked if they could help and volunteered to live there and help us, even when we did not have the resources to pay them.

We also could not have known that a few years after we opened the doors for retreatants that Rob would be diagnosed with a life-threatening illness that would become part of our life journey for the next ten years. While his cancer returned again and again, Rob, sustained by our spiritual life, the love of others, and great medical and holistic care, made it through this narrow passage of life and today is cancer-free and healthy. Our story is similar to the stories of others that have come to GilChrist to rest, heal, and deepen their connection to themselves and their spiritual practices to traverse these very challenging times.

We, like others, who respond to a call are asked to trust something larger, an unknowable force. When we trust in this intuitive knowing, there is a deep reverence for mystery that invites us to follow a course even when it does not make sense to the rational part of our mind. The creation of GilChrist drove us deeper into knowing what is most important in life: that how one lives in the world with light, compassion, joy, and love are what is most essential. We also learned that we cannot control many things in our lives, that we do not row the boats of our lives. This was fortunate, as we would have ended up somewhere else and not been taken out to sea and back home anew, grateful for the journey and the gift of grace. One of the unforeseen gifts of grace was being led to build a stone chapel.

Stone chapel

Chapter 2

A Chapel Is Born

"Do stones feel? Do they love their life?
Or does their patience drown out everything else?"

—MARY OLIVER
Blue Horses[1]

"In the Ojibwe language, nouns are animate or inanimate; the word for stone,
asin, is animate. One might think that stones have no actual power—after all,
we throw them, build with them, pile them, slice them. But who is to say that
the stones aren't using us to assert themselves? To transform themselves? One
day, the things we made out of stone may be all that's left of our species."

—LOUISE ERDRICH
"Louise Erdrich on the Power of Stones"[2]

Rob and I had traveled to monasteries and sacred sites in Scotland and Italy that were inspired by the stone structures and the little chapel of St. Francis of Assisi. Having Scottish/Celtic roots, I had been drawn, like many, to the mystery of ancient stone sites and why the oldest cultures in the world felt that stones had the power to heal and transform lives. It was hard to imagine who built some of the stone circles in Scotland thousands of years ago, but still, I could see why so many people made pilgrimages there and to the chapel that Francis built stone by stone in the 1500s, and how this led to a worldwide order of monks following the Franciscan way of life.

We had hoped someday that we could have a small stone chapel on the land at GilChrist but did not know how this would ever come about as we had only a small amount of field stone on our property and not enough money to pay a stone mason. Little did we know that very soon we would find someone to help us.

It was a fateful day when a woman, named Molly, appeared in the field of GilChrist as we were beginning to build. She had been sent by a friend at Apple Farm, the neighboring Jungian community, who heard we were looking for someone to help with a stone project. They knew Molly would be the perfect person as she had worked as a stonemason at one point in her life.

Molly asked what I hoped to create, and I told her possibly a bench and an altar in a garden to honor all mothers and the feminine spirit of the land. I expressed that someday maybe we could build a small stone chapel. With her indomitable spirit, she said, "Let's get started on building a chapel today."

I could not fathom how this might happen; we had few resources and only a used golf cart to transport stone, water, and mortar out to the field. There was no electricity so we would have to mix the mortar by hand. We had no knowledge of how to build anything. She was undeterred and said, "Let's go get the bags of mortar, five-gallon bottles of water, a wheelbarrow, and a few tools."

And so it began, collecting stones from our field and one of our farm neighbors and hauling it all in Tiger Lily, our golf cart. I, with Molly's help, was supposed to become the stonemason, and Rob would become the tender, which is the name for the person who assists. We were uncertain how this could be possible, but Molly inspired us to believe that it could be done and to trust that we could do it. She and others she knew would come to help.

The summer was one of the hottest in twenty-five years, and with nine hours of laying stone, the days were long. Trying to lift a stone by yourself and hold it while putting enough mortar in to hold the stone was difficult and dangerous, if not done very slowly and with careful attention. After laying the stone, you have to wait several hours for the mortar to dry and then come back to the chapel to cut and smooth it out before sunset. There were many times that I desperately did not want to go back, my muscles aching and exhausted, but I knew the mortar would be ruined if I did not.

In addition to laying stone every day, I found myself reading about the history of stone, looking at stonework everywhere I went, dreaming about stones and talking about stones with all of my friends, family, and people I hardly knew. People were patient and kind in listening to me go on about my passion for stone. One night, after a long day of laying stone, Rob was going to the

Laying of stones

store to pick up some groceries for dinner and as he was going out the door he said, "Do you need any mortar for the spaghetti?" He meant tomato sauce, but it was an easy mistake to make after nine hours of working with mortar that day. It was a sign of how immersed we were in the stone building process.

There were good days when some women would come unexpectedly, taking time out of their busy lives, driving often from a distance, to help, to feel that something they were doing was meaningful and that they could come in the future to be in the chapel and touch the stones they laid. If a handful of people came, we could sometimes lay a quarter-ton or more of stone in a day.

There were many other days when I was working alone, and I was only able to lay ten stones in nine hours of work. It requires patience and mindfulness every step of the way, and the injuries can be severe if one is not careful lifting or dropping the stones. I had no idea if we would find enough stone or how much we would need, but I just kept going with the help and encouragement of others, particularly Molly.

I was being changed by the experience building with stone in ways that I could not fully know at that point. The patience required was a challenge, and we didn't know if it would hold together or if we would ever finish the chapel in our lifetime. We had no idea what would emerge, what shape the building would be, the size or design. I had never worked on a project without a goal or vision. But simply in cooperation and service to a larger process, our trust was reinforced by every person who came to help and all of the encouragement from others to keep going. Like other dreams in life, knowing that the important thing was to believe it could happen also helped.

Stones are ancient and have powerful energy in their own right. Ancient cultures all over the world worshipped and built altars of stones and believed they had healing powers.

Stonework is a great lesson in imperfection. It is not like brick work with linear lines and level rows. Stonework is random, uneven, and unstructured. It is a very intuitive process. The miracle, as Molly taught me, is that the stone finds its own way to harmony.

Molly was like one of the quirky, enigmatic characters in the books she loved. Growing up in a home overflowing with books as the daughter of one of the most illustrious professors of English and History at Notre Dame, Molly lived in a little stone house and worked for those who were marginalized. She lived at the edge of the mainstream with little income as well. Molly had been many things in her life: a teacher, an artist, a counselor, a stonemason, but most of all, a free spirit following her own unique path in life.

What I could not have foreseen was that since Molly lived on the margins, her car would often break down for weeks at a time, and she could not make the trip from South Bend to Three Rivers. Molly had such a wide array of friends from every walk of life—artists, spiritual seekers, and families—that she knew and would encourage them to come help with the chapel.

Our circle of friends and friends from the neighboring spiritual communities came too and spread the word to their friends. So many people became part of the story of the stone chapel over many months, and stone by stone, the little chapel began to take shape. People would come to put a stone in for their family members, living and dead. One woman, Carolyn, put stones in for her entire Italian family. She continued to come help with landscaping around the hermitages, making a beautiful altar out of bent twigs. Other people came from the surrounding areas of Michigan and Indiana as the story grew about the little chapel that needed help.

The mason doing the brick and stonework on the buildings for GilChrist was named Cal, a soft spoken man and extraordinary brick layer. A gentle, kind person, his assistants had such respect for him. He would patiently answer my questions while building the chapel, like, "Why is an angle iron needed to build the fireplace and where do I get one?" He was a third-generation brick-and-stone layer, and all of the workers came because they had such admiration for Cal and Rick, who was our builder. Rick was a lay minister and also a builder, donating half of his work life to Habitat for Humanity and other charitable projects. The workers that came because of him were all special in their own right and men of great faith. They gave more then we

could afford to pay them and felt the importance of the place and the chapel. They donated extra time and were kind and helpful.

One day, I asked Cal to come to the chapel to see if I had put the two hexagonal windows and sandstone-slab window ledge in properly before I finished going around them with stone. I did not want to have to tear out the work I had already done if they were not even. He asked if I had a level. I did not even know what that was and had just been going by intuition. So Cal pulled a small level and string out of his work belt and measured them; astoundingly, they were perfectly level. I was ecstatic and he kindly gave me his level, which his father had given to him. I treasure this gift to this day.

At first, Cal and the other workers were not sure if I was serious about building the chapel and thought I would give up. But after many weeks watching me in the heat every day and all the hours we were working, they knew how much it meant to me and how devoted I was to trying to build it.

We did not know that Cal's wife had been sick during the building process and was dying of cancer. Cal told us after the chapel was built and asked if he could bring her there, as she had not left their house in many weeks and wanted to see it before she died. This was a wish that he granted for her. I only hope it brought them some peace in the process.

A man that lived in the neighborhood named Carrie heard the story of GilChrist and the chapel. He came to volunteer, like so many others. He helped me lay the brick floor and did beautiful stone work when we were too tired. Molly's spirit was always present even when she was not, then unexpectedly she would come walking over the hill, sleeves rolled up and ready to work.

One time when Molly came and we were working side by side laying stone, she picked up a small, sharp piece of stone and started impulsively carving something on the flat face of a stone over the fireplace. I was mortaring a large stone and not paying much attention until she stopped and gasped. "Oh no," she said, "I don't know why I just did that."

I quit working and came over to look at a Celtic cross carved on the face of the stone. It seemed impossible she could do it so perfectly symmetrical. She kept apologizing for not asking permission. This, like all the offerings people gave when they came to help, was a grace beyond imagination. Little did I or anyone else know that was the last time Molly was able to come to the chapel and that I would see her. She did not know at the time she had cancer and was diagnosed shortly afterwards, sadly dying months later. We all felt an even greater urgency to honor Molly's memory by working harder. I felt her spirit then, and it still permeates the chapel to this day.

In the months that followed, people appeared to help. Tom—a friend of Molly's and the person that taught her to be a stonemason and got her a job laying stone when she needed work—brought his family, who had built their own stone house together. Molly had told them the story of the chapel. Tom was a gruff man who spoke few words. He looked at the small stones we had remaining in a pile and said we did not have a keystone and could not finish the arch over the door without one.

The keystone is the last stone to put in, anchoring the adjacent stones so they don't fall. It has to be of a perfect size and symmetry to fit the stones around it.

I drove him around the land in Tiger Lily. He saw the edge of a stone embedded in the dirt and told me to stop. I did, and he took his mallet with him and pounded the earth around it to reveal a perfect size keystone to place over the door. When we pounded the plywood out that was supporting the arch in the door, I was amazed to see that the keystone held the arch in place perfectly.

One beautiful fall day, Rob and I stood in the middle of the chapel and looked up, hardly believing that the walls were now over our heads. With tears of gratitude and elation, we both said, "This is enough, our work is done," knowing intuitively that it was time to let others come and see it. We thought this endeavor would take a lifetime, if we could do it at all. It was no longer a dream, but a reality. Now it was time for our builder, Rick, to figure out how to make a roof and a door that would fit a structure so uneven and imperfect with odd angles. We had no idea how difficult this would be, but he—with the help of some workers—devoted as many months fashioning the roof and door for the little chapel as it took for us to build it.

Radiant light

> *"To the pilgrim who breaks his journey to come in and pray, they offer shy yet beautiful light that restores your seeing. And you remember who you are."*
>
> —JOHN O'DONOHUE
> *Beauty: The Invisible Embrace*[3]

People from all walks of life found their way through the dense pine forest to the little chapel. They came to heal, to prepare to die, to celebrate, to commemorate, and to bless. They planted trees around the chapel for children born, for parents who had died, for their marriage or partner ceremony or ritual. They left notes and messages, buried in the caverns in between the stones, and even a wedding ring long after a divorce.

They lit candles, built fires, and slept on the floor for comfort when in despair. They prayed, meditated, played music, and sang songs that filled the chapel with their longing, desires, and hopes. They left parts of themselves, their breath, gifts, and blessings; and they took small stones from the floor to remember. They came from all walks of life: some people we knew, many we did not, and sometimes unexpected visits from well-known people, like Desmond Tutu. They still come now without ceasing and in the future, when all else is gone and it's only the stones still there, people will wonder why and who put them there. This will be part mystery and part miracle. We are still, to this day, filled with awe and gratitude that we, along with so many others, were able to construct this chapel into creation, one that will bring comfort, peace, joy, and hope to so many even after we are not on this earth.

Meditating in the Interfaith Gardens

Chapter 3:

A Sense of the Sacred

"Listen carefully and attend with the ear of the heart."

—Michael Casey
The Road to Eternal Life:
Reflections on the Prologue of Benedict's Rule[1]

People followed their hearts to come to GilChrist. They came from all walks of life and many different faiths: Christian, Buddhist, Hindu, Jewish, Native American, and even those that did not have any faith belief. They came in times of exhaustion, grief, loss of meaning, creativity, and loss of hope; seeking a place of retreat, rest, and healing. They courageously left their everyday lives to follow the small voice inside, trying to remember who they are and what is essential. They also came in time of celebration, commemoration, and threshold moments.

What they found is a place for communion and contemplation, where they can be alone or with others as they seek to recover a sense of the sacred. In the silence and simplicity of the land, the hermitages, and the chapel, they slowly return to their true selves and feel a sense of homecoming. They bring their gifts of longing and intention. As the hours and the days go by, they begin to listen to the wind, the sounds of the prairie grass, the trees and creatures abounding in the fields, and they feel held and blessed.

> "A blessing is a circle of light drawn around a person to protect, heal, and strengthen. A blessing does not foreshadow, it brightens the way. When a blessing is invoked a window opens to the eternal."
>
> —JOHN O'DONOHUE
> *To Bless the Space Between Us: A Book of Blessings*[2]

They walked the labyrinth, the paths. They sat in prayer and contemplation, living like monastics of various traditions, inhabiting their small hermitages alone but connected to others.

"The Laura is a colony of hermits living in separate solitary dwellings (hermitages) surrounding a central chapel and common house."

—Eugene L. Romano
A Way of Desert Spirituality: The Rule of Life of the Hermits of Bethlehem of the Heart of Jesus[3]

Coming home to your heart

Slowing down and sinking into a natural, quiet rhythm, the body begins to recover a feeling of rest. We have lost the meaning of the word "rest" and the profound healing effect it has in our lives. In a society that values productivity, speed, and efficiency, rest has become less and less part of our daily lives. Rest is not merely the absence of being busy, it has a quality of safety and comfort and implies trust at a deep level of our being. The inward place of rest is undemanding, gentle, merciful, and kind. We sink into rest, surrender, and let go of effort. Rest is clarifying, refreshing like a cool stream of water and fresh air. Rest returns us to our inner rhythm and affirms our intuitive wisdom. It reassures us that we have a way of knowing which will tell us what we need, when we need it.

When we rest, time seems to stand still and teaches us that the world can go on without us. We begin to recognize that we are a speck of dust in the hands of time. The paradox of this experience of insignificance is the feeling of being part of a larger web of creation, never in isolation. Rest brings us the understanding that there is unity in all things. The Christians speak of this as "rest in God;" the Greeks used the word *hesychia* to describe the process of resting the heart in prayer. The Buddhist tradition refers to resting in the experience of the moment. This experience can cause our perception of time to change and feel like elongated moments, enhancing our sensual capacities of sight, sound, taste, and touch. Throughout history, all major religious traditions have used fasting—a rest from food—to enhance our spiritual sensitivity. Fasting can also imply rest from other activities like speaking, as the word fasting comes from the Hebrew word *tsum,* which means "to shut one's mouth." The deeper meaning of fasting is to rest the body and mind so that our spiritual capacities may be enhanced.

Recovering the meaning of rest in our lives is important preparation for times of illness and the dying process. It teaches us the value of patience, timing, and how to honor the cycles and seasons of life. It helps us hold ourselves and others gently in times of fragility and transition. If we could rest more in each other's arms, hold each other more, our relationships could help heal the world. We would listen more and feel a greater sense of interconnectedness and compassion. The world would be a better place for all of us and all of creation.

Reflections in the garden

Windhill—a place to meet and share

Chapter 4

Communion

"The deepest level of communication is not communication, but communion.
It is wordless. It is beyond words. It is beyond speech. It is beyond concept.
Not that we discover a new unity, but we discover an old unity."

—THOMAS MERTON
The Hidden Ground of Love: The Letters of Thomas Merton on Religious Experience and Social Concerns [1]

Rarely do we find ourselves in a place not only steeped in stillness but also in communion, where we can feel a deep connection with others without words. People that find their way to GilChrist gravitate to certain hermitages, coming over and over again through the years. They feel a sense of attachment as if the space is animate and they have a deep bond with the place. I placed journals in all of the hermitages with the hopes that we would have a sense of how the time of retreat would be for those that came.

The journals also served as a way for retreatants to process their experience and share it with others that would be coming to read the entries and write their own. We had no idea how important these would become and how retreatants would share their experience and their lives through poems, drawings, objects in nature, and beautiful recordings. Now, after so many years, there are hundreds of journal entries in each of the hermitages, connecting each person to a stream of human stories similar to their own, letting them know that their struggles, sorrows, and confusion are universal.

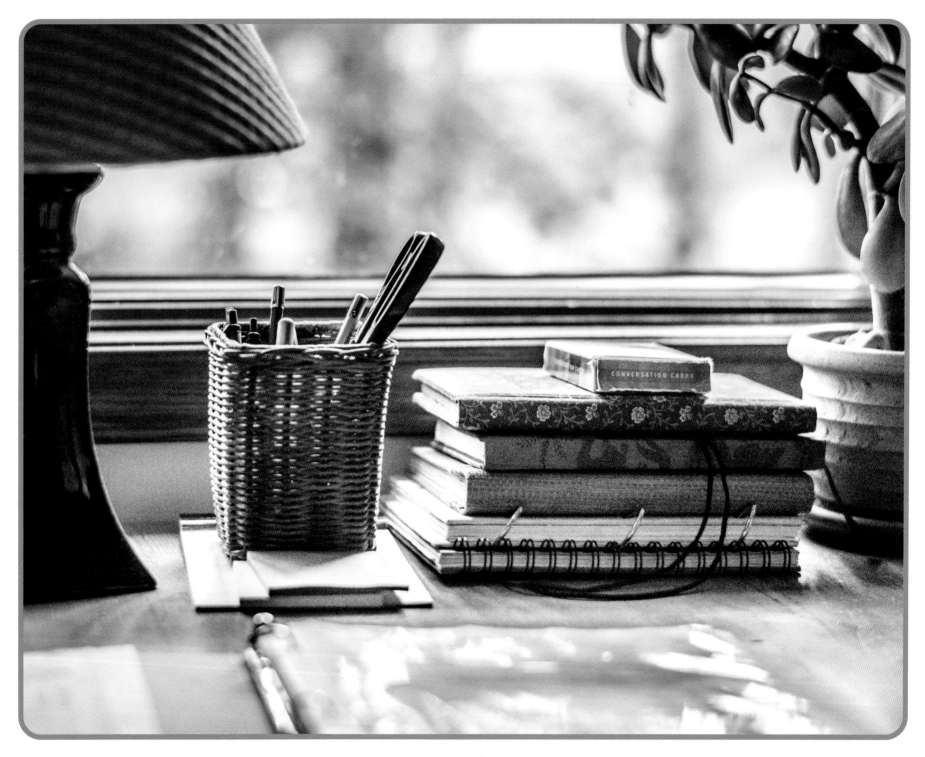

Journals

This is one of those entries:

I feel compelled as I prepare this space for you to welcome you "home," whether it is your first time at GilChrist or to someone who may have stayed in this hermitage many times. The weather has been cold, strong winds, but warm in this little house, and the sense of peace is "thick." I prepare the hermitage now in your honor in the hope that your retreat from the world gives you strength to return. If I have left something undone, forgive me. It was my arrogance, not my heart that leaves it so. I hope you find joy, I hope you find peace. I hope you find what you came here for.

With care,
The one who was here last

The blessings they leave behind are part of a collective memory that shines a light for those who will come to GilChrist in the future and is a seed for when they return again. They share their poems, drawings, and objects from nature. What they write from the heart calls to the hearts of the ones that follow.

Here is another journal entry from one of our retreatants that impacted those who followed (September 2010).

> *On a dark, rainy afternoon in late September 2010, I found myself in a very dark, unsettled place in my life. On the edge of burnout from a job that was consuming my energy, time, and the creative places in my soul, I longed to be any place but the cramped, limited space of my tiny Chicago apartment. I needed to go somewhere to connect with something life giving and numinous— yet within my reach.*
>
> *I found myself driving to a retreat center, and despite the fact I was unfamiliar with the driving route and uncertain about taking two whole days off work, setting off alone to a "remote and unknown place," my curiosity compelled me forward. This decision was confirmed when I hit the gravel road leading to Windhill and the single word 'GilChrist' at the entrance. I was welcomed by a woman in a golf cart and taken to my hermitage and felt that I had come home.*
>
> *My experiences at GilChrist over the past nine years have shown me the way to essential wisdom and personal healing. In the midst of the challenges like burnout, fears, death, and the "What do I do now?" moments, I have learned to always seek solitude in a place of beauty and silence—for there, in the here and now, lies the answers and the healing.*

A place of healing: Tree of Life

In 2019 before the COVID-19 pandemic, on the twenty-fifth anniversary of GilChrist, we held a series of storytelling sessions where people were invited back to GilChrist to tell us how they found their way there, what happened during their time, and what they took away from the experience. If they could not come, they were invited to send us what they wanted to share.

This is one of the many heartrending stories that was shared by a woman, Allison. She is a storyteller and musician who has come to GilChrist for twenty years. She would write, compose songs, walk the labyrinth and the paths, rest, and reset. She came in times of important decisions, to decide whether to marry, whether to have a child, and then again with her newborn baby boy.

The following story was of a time she came at a dark and desperate moment in her life. She had a rare form of melanoma that did not have a treatment at the time of her diagnosis and had less than a 20 percent chance of living. Her cancer had advanced from stage 2 to stage 4 and metastasized to many other organs, including her brain. After repeated courses of chemotherapy, radiation, and brain surgery, the cancer was still spreading rapidly.

A new clinical trial was starting in several cities in the country with a protocol for her type of cancer. Allison went to all of the sites for consultations and the doctors encouraged her try the treatment. If she didn't, she would have less than three to five months to live. This was a most difficult decision as to whether it was worth going forward, not knowing what kind of quality of life she would have with her family and also knowing some people had not survived the treatment. She had one week to make the decision and decided to come to GilChrist to walk the labyrinth and the paths, to sit in silence and solitude to try to listen to her heart and find clarity. The staff was vigilant about checking on her, and her family was supportive of her choice to go to a hermitage in the woods. She decided to have the treatment, which put her in remission. Fortunately, Allison has been cancer-free since 2017.

One of her times coming on retreat in between her chemo and radiation treatments, Allison saw a bird on the feeder outside her window in the hermitage and felt compelled to compose a song symbolizing an awakening into a deeper feeling of inner freedom. It is a song of hope, courage, and beauty. After she shared this story with a group of us at GilChrist, she picked up her guitar to play the song she wrote. The poignancy of the lyrics and the beauty of her voice was an overwhelmingly moving and inspiring experience.

The gift of people sharing their journeys through loss and grief is precious as they help light the way for others. They teach us that in loving fully, we will also at times endure great grief. They help us know the truth that there are times when we cannot control our fate, but we always have a choice on how to come into relationship with it. This is the greatest act of human dignity.

Journey through the labyrinth

Brandon's story is another one of finding peace and beauty amidst a time of unfathomable challenges. He found his way to GilChrist as part of a teacher's residency program, a partnership with the Yeager Family Foundation and the Fetzer Institute. The program was created for elementary school teachers around the country to provide a week-long retreat in the summers for rest and renewal as well as a way to be with other teachers and share their stories in a reflective setting. The teachers could participate in activities like mindfulness, creative arts, labyrinth walks, and storytelling. Over the last eighteen years, a number of teachers have returned many times, including third-grade teacher Brandon. His is a transformative story of finding peace and joy while battling a very rare and aggressive form of cancer.

Brandon was diagnosed in 2016 when he was thirty-six; he has been through fifteen surgeries and seven rounds of chemotherapy and anticipates more chemo when he is strong enough to tolerate the treatments. Brandon is also a classical pianist and naturalist devoted to growing butterfly habitats and teaching his students about monarchs. He provides each student in his third-grade class with a mason jar containing a caterpillar. They learn to care for the butterfly and feed it milkweed until it becomes a chrysalis and is eventually ready to be released. Brandon believes that what he experienced in practicing mindfulness, having the support of others, and being immersed in nature at GilChrist allowed him to find peace amidst the uncertainty of his health challenges. It also gave him the ability to bring these experiences to his students, teaching them mindfulness and taking them out into the natural world. He has witnessed a change in their ability to learn and be calm with adding a greater perspective to their daily lives. His enthusiasm for life touches everyone around him, especially his five-year-old daughter whom he brings to GilChrist and other places in nature as often as possible.

Brandon feels one of the greatest gifts from his times at GilChrist is his connection to the staff and other teachers. They are an extended family, accompanying and supporting him on the arduous journey. He is an inspiration and a light, touching the lives of so many others in his time on the earth.

These stories of healing are only a few of the ones we have witnessed and are sharing here, as so many people have found their way to GilChrist over the years and keep coming back over and over again. The journals, with their multitude of stories, are now many volumes. I remember years ago when I was leading a weekend retreat at GilChrist, one of the activities we did the first morning was to draw a picture that represented an important event, and I asked if anyone would like to explain their picture or, if they felt like it, act it out in some way. I will never forget the scene when one of the women whose husband had just left her drew a picture of a big heart and then proceeded to rip it into shreds, laying the pieces all over the room. Spontaneously, she began to move and dance, picking up each little piece and with her own saliva mended the heart back together. The whole group was in tears as we witnessed this poignant act of human dignity and survival.

The universal themes of loss, grief, letting go, and survival are expressed in so many of the stories we've seen unfold. They are the stories of all of our lives; everyone is touched by grief at some point.

What calls us back to life is often a confluence of factors—ultimately a journey of humility and acceptance of mystery and grace. The journeys of these individuals are like a fragile shell, one that is held together by a thin membrane through the extraordinary force of the ocean waves. It is the message that they bring back from the journey that helps light the way for others and teaches us what is essential in this lifetime. These experiences and emotions call us to courageously live fully all of the moments and seasons of our lives.

The retreatants often take small objects from the land and hermitages or small stones from the chapel to carry back to their homes. This helps them to remember that they can return again and again as the cycles and seasons of their lives change or they feel their inner light beginning to dim.

Transformation

Pathway to healing

Chapter 5

Returning Home

*"Make yourself familiar with the angels and behold them frequently in spirit;
for without being seen, they are present with you."*

—ST. FRANCIS DE SALES[1]

The slow journey back home after an experience out of time in silence is a process: one reluctantly tries to let go of an invisible thread holding part of themselves that is still anchored in the land and place. It takes time to reenter the speed and noise of the world. Revisiting the memories, images, and sensations of their experiences, they try to integrate the lessons they learned back into their everyday lives. They hold on to the desire to keep alive the sense of the sacred, to listen to their hearts and take care of their body, mind, and soul, bringing the spirit of GilChrist into their relationships and work.

People often continue the practices of mindfulness and contemplation they learned at GilChrist and will share these with others. They have a greater commitment to tending to their inner psychological and spiritual life on a daily basis. Some use journals while others prefer rituals, like walking in nature each day, reading books on contemplative awareness, or practicing traditions that help sustain them in the busyness and complexities of daily life. They also find support in others that are kindred spirits to help each other. Some of the people they have met during their time at GilChrist continue to be part of their lives, encouraging them along the way.

We do ultimately get swept back up into the whirlwind of life around us, but all is not lost. The memory is still there, the invisible thread still tethered to the place in our heart and soul. People return month after month, year after year, for a short time or a longer stay, when they hear the call whisper to them once again. Some find they are not ready to return back to the world and will stay for extended periods of time. Some come for a month at a time every year. Others bring their friends and family with them to help them understand the benefits of a time of retreat and reconnection to a greater simplicity and nature together. Parents bring their children for milestones in their lives to celebrate, using rituals they create. They often work in the garden or on the land planting trees, feeling a sense of connection to the place and knowing they can come again to see the fruits of their labor.

As time passes, they come again to celebrate the transitions in their lives like special anniversaries, getting married, having a child, changing careers, and other milestones. They also come to commemorate the loss of a loved one in their lives, burying ashes, planting flowers, and other rituals to honor those that they have lost.

They go out into the world, bringing the effects of their experiences to those around them. They are like the great Yew tree that has "the ability to regenerate through downward-hanging limbs that root in the ground to form new trees."[2] Each person leaving GilChrist is like a newly rooted tree taking their light and wisdom with them on their journey, which touches the lives of many to help heal the world around them.

Caring for the earth

Path toward the light

Epilogue

"The final stage of the wisdom journey in mythology is symbolized by the ruling image of the king or queen or what I like to call the grandfather or grandmother."

—RICHARD ROHR[1]

As we enter into old age, we are now the grandmother and grandfather coming home after a busy work life to survey the landscape of our lives. This is a time of retrospection and the chapter of letting go of old ways of doing and being. We, like so many others, cannot fathom how fast time has passed. As Rob is turning eighty and I seventy, it is hard to remember when we were forty-seven and thirty-seven embarking on this unimagined journey.

Many of the people who inspired us to make a quarter-turn in our life path have since passed on to the other side. They are with us now in spirit as we cross this threshold into the final chapter. Helen Luke of the Apple Farm Community wrote in her book, *Old Age*:

> *"Here are the proper occupations of old age: prayer,*
> *which is the quickening of the mind, the rooting of*
> *the attention in the ground of being; song, which*
> *is the expression of spontaneous joy in the harmony*
> *of chaos; the 'telling of old tales,' which among all*
> *primitives was the supreme function of the old."*[2]

There is an urgency to try to tell the old tales, hoping that it may inspire others to follow their dreams and trust their hearts.

Looking back, everything often feels like a dream; some parts of it are fading, some we want to forget or reframe. Yet our task is to accept the joys, sufferings, regrets and to claim the wholeness of the life journey. As Florida Scott-Maxwell says in her book written at the end of her life:

"You need only claim the events of your life to make yourself yours. When you truly possess all you have been and done, which may take some time, you are fierce with reality." [3]

Accepting reality and letting go of self-importance, of what we may not finish in life, and allowing others to pick up the pieces to do in their lifetime is the ladder to humility. In Monastic traditions, the "Ladder of Humility" goes down—the time of laying down the burdens of too muchness, too many things, too many worries, and too many struggles to control the events of our lives. It is a time to trust in the larger mystery that we cannot see or fully know. Our lives may get smaller as we lose the ability to do the things we could do earlier in life, and this requires us to bring greater awareness and creativity to our days, to focus our precious energy on the beauty and abundance around us.

You can see in the faces of some people at the last stage of life a light in their eyes, a childlike spontaneity and wonder that emanates out into the world around them. They have an inner freedom to be lighter, more compassionate, and patient. This is the journey to simplicity in our souls, to remember what is essential. As the Psalm says, "Lord let me know the shortness of life so that I may gain wisdom of heart." [4]

We could not have imagined the condition of our world as we approach 2023: that we would be living with the effects of a pandemic, surrounded by divisions in our society, and witnessing the accelerating destruction of our planet. It is heartbreaking to bear witness to the level of aggression and inhumanity around the world. Although this has been true throughout history, somehow in our arrogance, we did not think it would be in our lifetime.

A place for communion

Trying to find a way to build a relationship with our struggles can at times seem overwhelming and prove difficult not to fall into despair, anger, and hopelessness. Now more than ever, the need to find a way to our light within and our ground of being is essential. Not surprisingly, millions of people are seeking ways to find peace and perspective through mindfulness, meditation, prayer, and other modalities. They are migrating to places in nature, retreat centers, monasteries, and sacred sites. There is a renewed impulse to reflect on the meaning of life and how to live simpler and with greater harmony within themselves and with others around them.

The only thing people have to offer to the world is our presence and our efforts to bring healing. If our actions come from a place of anger and fear, we will contribute to the darkness. If we come from a place of peace, compassion, and love, we can be part of the healing process.

Thomas Merton states it this way:

> *"Those of us who attempt to act and do things for others or for the world without deepening our own self-understanding, freedom, integrity, and capacity to love, will not have anything to give others. We will communicate to them nothing but the contagion of our own obsessions, our aggressivity, our ego-centered ambitions, our delusions about ends and means."*[5]

As companions on this journey, walking hand in hand and heart to heart, we can be beacons of light in the storm. The presence of luminosity has the power to change the world. One light can spread out to all around them—a brilliant star. They can help us remember there is something larger, a light beyond us that connects us all. May we be blessed with courage and passion to move forward on this miraculous life journey.

Love and devotion

Giving thanks

Acknowledgments

This section of the book could be longer than the book itself, as there are so many people that became part of a village to care for GilChrist: the land, buildings, and all of the people that have come over the last many years. People brought their talents, creativity, and devotion to an unfolding miracle. There are many hands now holding GilChrist, blessing each person who comes there. In the future, I am confident there will be many more who will come to help.

I will attempt to shine a light on those that have been part of the process, while knowing there are so many we will never know that helped along the way.

We could not possibly have created GilChrist without Rick Leland, our builder, and his wife, Nancy. His generosity of spirit and time has its imprint on every building. We also owe a great debt to all of the workers that helped him.

Thank you to Jay Fishman, who helped the dream of GilChrist become a reality.

Patrick and Celeste Jones came early on as the first caretakers, followed by John Howie and Paula Andrassi, who have stayed through thick and thin. John continues to provide counsel and teaches mindfulness for many that come seeking greater peace and perspective in their lives.

A friend and neighbor, Deborah Yeager, became part of GilChrist, bringing her beautiful presence and hospitality to care for others. Her work to support the teachers in the residency program with her family foundation has been a great gift.

Chris Smith brought a vision and an awareness early on of the sacred energies amidst the land that was significant.

We want to thank our resident hermit in the farm down the road, Nancy Bell, for her gifts of wisdom and ways of knowing and seeing that helped to open our eyes and ears to the spirits around us.

Our deepest gratitude to all the hands and hearts that helped build the chapel, plant trees, and tend the land: Carolyn Kelly, Molly Sullivan, Carrie, and all of the groups that came to help out and left more than we could have ever imagined.

In deep appreciation to the Fetzer Institute for their ongoing support of GilChrist. The Institute staff that have come to volunteer each year, making the place beautiful for others. Tim Jones, who oversaw all of the operations, provided guidance and support to keep GilChrist sustained and growing. Amy Furguson, who helps communicate the mission and beauty of GilChrist and who is also deeply appreciated for her encouragement and help with the book at different stages.

For all their work to support GilChrist and the community of Three Rivers, we want to thank Kirstin and Rob Vander Giessen-Reitsma. Kirstin has been helpful in so many ways to make the book possible—taking photographs with her contemplative eye for beauty and capturing the essence of the GilChrist experience. Deborah Haak's help for finding the individuals/photographers (Fran Dwight, Laurie Pruitt, Elizabeth Coleman, Colette Heusinkveld, Paula Hattan, Michele Gossman, Michael Rice, and the man with the kite and the camera that took the amazing aerial views of the Labryinth) and accessing the photographs that are included in the book helped make this book a beautiful expression of GilChrist.

Presently, we are gifted with the caretakers Kirstin, John, Gail, Deborah, Johnathan, and Erika. Each of their special gifts make it possible for GilChrist to continue to flourish. We want to thank them for all they have done and know they will be joined by others in the future to keep the miracle alive.

Our immense gratitude to the surrounding communities, their commitment to contemplative traditions, and the work of inner transformation and prayer. St. Gregory's Abbey inspired us to follow the Benedictine Rule and build GilChrist and Apple Farm with their commitment to the inner work of integration through dreamwork and reflection. Our unexpected friendships with Helen Luke and others became a source of nourishment and support for our own work.

Naomi and David Wenger at the Hermitage, a Mennonite retreat center, your devotion to sustain a place for contemplation, prayer, and spiritual direction is inspiring.

Ruth and Vic Eichler came to live on the adjacent land, bringing many gifts and building the Earth Song Peace Chamber, a place others could come to experience the sacred sounds of the earth and connect with other sacred sound sites around the world.

To all of the people that made difficult decisions to move and live around all of these communities, leaving their professional lives from many parts of the country because of their commitment to a simpler life devoted to deeper spiritual values—thank you.

There are too many to mention, but we want to remember and thank those who have passed on, like our dear friend Joanne Holden, owner of the Long Lake Bookstore. Joanne was a legend in the area and provided a place important to all of the surrounding communities. The store was as unique as she was.

We want to honor fully Helen Luke, the heart of the Apple Farm community, a great Jungian writer that Laurens van der Post said was the greatest feminine voice of the last century.

I would like to acknowledge Caroline Whiting, another person that followed a call to leave her life in New York and come to live as part of the Apple Farm Community. She has helped make this book possible from the beginning and inspires aspiring writers with her graciousness and indomitable spirit.

Our Cistercian friends have been a constant source of inspiration and guidance. A number have gone beyond, but we remain grateful for the continued friendship with Father Brendan and Sister GilChrist.

My friend Nathalie Kees has been here from the beginning, helping to create GilChrist and this book. The gift of our friendship is beyond measure, and I cannot thank you enough.

Other women friends who were part of the process, before it was even a dream, that deserve a special thank you are Elizabeth Coleman and Mary Hamilton.

To retreatants like Hope Kerr and many others that come month after month and year after year with their commitment to living a contemplative life, inspiring others to live this way in their own life.

Thank you Allison Downey, Brandon Bear, and Linda Plamondon for sharing your stories of hope and courage.

My dear friends Terry Helwig and Sue Monk Kidd have been a source of continuing inspiration and encouragement for writing.

To Milli and all the staff at Brown Books Publishing Group. Thank you to my editors Olivia, Carissa, and Sterling. I would also like to thank Danny Whitworth for his amazing work bringing GilChrist to life in the design of this book. A special gratitude for Brittany Griffiths and all her efforts to bring this book through the process and into publication.

And finally, to Rob, my husband, as we approach thirty-two years since the fateful trip to Three Rivers. We found each other along the way and have been held and carried by a larger force to live out our life and love together. I am grateful we did not know what would be required of us and said a resounding "Yes" to take the leap.

In Norway they have a saying for gratitude, "*tusen takk*," which means "a thousand thanks." This is exactly how we feel about the whole process and the people that made it possible.

Molly and Rob at GilChrist today

Notes

Preface

1. William Stafford, *The Way It Is: New & Selected Poems* (Saint Paul, Minnesota: Graywolf Press, 1998).
2. J.R.R. Tolkien, *The Lord of the Rings, The Return of the King* (London, England: George Allen & Unwin, 1955).
3. John O'Donohue, *Beauty: The Invisible Embrace* (New York: HarperCollins Publishers, 2004).
4. Anne Frank, *Anne Frank: The Diary of a Young Girl*, trans. B. M. Mooyaart (New York: DoubleDay & Co, 1952).

Chapter 1

1. Esther de Waal, *A Life-Giving Way: A Commentary on the Rule of St. Benedict* (Collegeville, Minnesota: Liturgical Press, 1995).
2. John O'Donohue, *To Bless the Space Between Us: A Book of Blessings,* 1st ed. (New York: Doubleday, 2008).

Chapter 2

1. Mary Oliver, *Blue Horses* (New York, New York: The Penguin Press, 2014).
2. Deborah Treisman, "Louise Erdrich on the Power of Stones," *The New Yorker*, September 2, 2019. https://www.newyorker.com/books/this-week-in-fiction/louise-erdrich-09-09-19.
3. John O'Donohue, *Beauty: The Invisible Embrace* (New York: HarperCollins Publishers, 2004).

Chapter 3

1. Michael Casey, *The Road to Eternal Life: Reflections on the Prologue of Benedict's Rule* (Collegeville, Minnesota: Liturgical Press, 2011).
2. John O'Donohue, *To Bless the Space Between Us: A Book of Blessings,* 1st ed. (New York: Doubleday, 2008).
3. Eugene L. Romano, *A Way of Desert Spirituality: The Rule of Life of the Hermits of Bethlehem of the Heart of Jesus* (New York: Alba House, 1992).

Chapter 4

1. Thomas Merton, *The Hidden Ground of Love: The Letters of Thomas Merton on Religious Experience and Social Concerns*, ed. William H. Shannon (New York: Farrar, Straus and Giroux, 2011).

Chapter 5

1. *Catholic Digest.* "St. Francis de Sales—Make Yourself Familiar with the Angels . . .," September 29, 2021. https://www.catholicdigest.com/amp/from-the-magazine/quiet-moment/st-francis-de-sales-make-yourself-familiar-with-the-angels-2/.
2. Diane Cook, Len Jenshel, and Verlyn Klinkenborg, *Wise Trees* (New York: Abrams, 2017).

Epilogue

1. Richard Rohr (OFM), "Daily Meditation: Becoming a Grand Parent," Center for Action and Contemplation, September 23, 2022. https://cac.org/daily-meditations/becoming-a-grand-parent-2022-09-23/.
2. Helen M. Luke, *Old Age: Journey into Simplicity* (Great Barrington, Massachusetts; Edinburgh, Scotland: Lindisfarne, 2010).
3. Florida Scott-Maxwell, *The Measure of My Days: One Woman's Vivid, Enduring Celebration of Life and Aging* (New York: Penguin Books, 1979).
4. *The Psalms: An Inclusive Language Version Based on the Grail Translation from the Hebrew* (Chicago, IL: GIA Publications, 1983).
5. Thomas Merton, *Thomas Merton, Spiritual Master: The Essential Writings,* ed. Lawrence Cunningham (New York: Paulist Press, 1992).